Life Under the Sea

Lobsters

by Cari Meister

Bullfrog
Books

Ideas for Parents and Teachers

Bullfrog Books let children practice reading informational text at the earliest reading levels. Repetition, familiar words, and photo labels support early readers.

Before Reading

- Ask the child to think about lobsters. Ask: What do you know about lobsters?
- Look at the picture glossary together. Read and discuss the words.

Read the Book

- "Walk" through the book and look at the photos. Let the child ask questions. Point out the photo labels.
- Read the book to the child, or have him or her read independently.

After Reading

- Prompt the child to think more. Ask: Can you think of other sea animals that have shells? How is a lobster like other animals? How is it different?

Bullfrog Books are published by Jump!
5357 Penn Avenue South
Minneapolis, MN 55419
www.jumplibrary.com

Library of Congress Cataloging-in-Publication Data

Meister, Cari, author.
 Lobsters / by Cari Meister.
    pages cm. — (Life under the sea)
  Summary: "This photo-illustrated book for early readers tells about the physical features of lobsters, how they catch food, and how they stay safe from predators. Includes picture glossary" — Provided by publisher.
  Audience: 5-8.
  Audience: Grade K to 3.
  Includes bibliographical references and index.
  ISBN 978-1-62031-099-1 (hardcover) —
  ISBN 978-1-62496-166-3 (ebook)
 1. Lobsters — Juvenile literature. I. Title.
II. Series: Bullfrog books. Life under the sea.
 QL444.M33M443 2015
 595.3'84—dc23
                                                    2013042377

Series Editor: Rebecca Glaser
Series Designer: Ellen Huber
Book Designer: Anna Peterson
Photo Researcher: Kurtis Kinneman

Photo Credits: All photos by Shutterstock except: Andrew J. Martinez/Science Source, 11, 12–13; Michele Hall / SeaPics.com, 14–15, 16–17, 23bl; OceanwideImages.com, 4, 5, 6–7

Printed in the United States of America at Corporate Graphics, in North Mankato, Minnesota.
6-2014
10 9 8 7 6 5 4 3 2 1

Table of Contents

A Lot of Legs

A lobster walks
on the ocean floor.

He has ten legs.

He has a hard shell.

It protects his body.

shell

He has long antennas.
They feel.
They smell for food.

antenna

Here comes a crab.

A lobster grabs it.

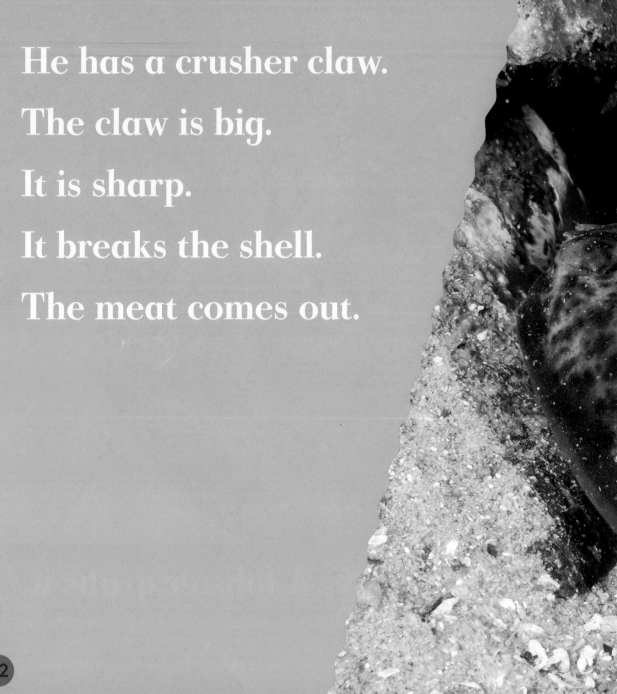

He has a crusher claw.

The claw is big.

It is sharp.

It breaks the shell.

The meat comes out.

meat

crusher claw

A lobster grows all its life.

It gets too big for its shell.

It molts.

The hard shell cracks off.

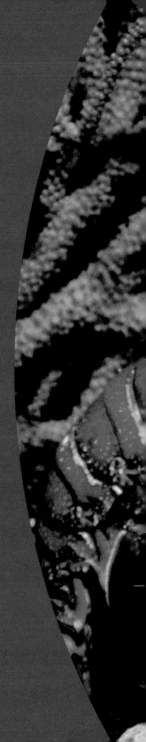

old
shell

The new shell is soft.

new
shell

In time, it gets hard.

Oh no!
A hungry sea turtle!

He wants dinner.

The lobster must hide.

Look!

There is a reef.

Now he is safe.

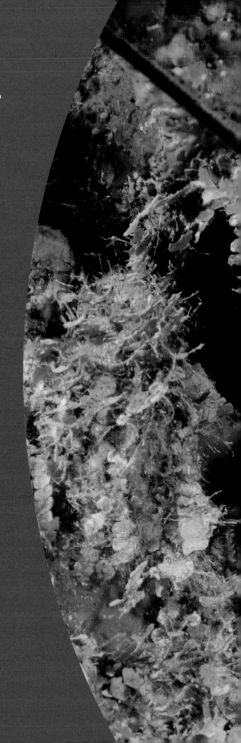

reef

Parts of a Lobster

shell
The outer part of a lobster that protects the inside parts.

eye
A lobster has eyes on stalks, but it cannot see very well.

antennas
Two long feelers on a lobster's head that help it smell and touch.

crusher claw
A big pincher on the largest leg of a lobster.

Picture Glossary

crab
A sea animal with a hard shell and eight legs.

ocean floor
The flat bottom of the sea.

molt
When an animal grows too big for its shell and breaks out of it.

reef
A strip of coral in shallow ocean water.

Index

To Learn More

Learning more is as easy as 1, 2, 3.

1) Go to www.factsurfer.com

2) Enter "lobsters" into the search box.

3) Click the "Surf" button to see a list of websites.

With factsurfer.com, finding more information is just a click away.